SUPER STEM CAREERS

A Day at Work with an
ASTRONOMER

DAVID LEE

PowerKiDS
press.

New York

Published in 2016 by The Rosen Publishing Group, Inc.
29 East 21st Street, New York, NY 10010

First Edition

Editor: Caitie McAneney
Book Design: Katelyn Heinle/Reann Nye

Photo Credits: Cover Stolk/Thinkstockphotos.com; cover, pp. 1, 3, 4, 6–12, 14–16, 18, 20, 22–24 (topographic vector design) Dancake/Shutterstock.com; p. 5 Valerio Pardi/Shutterstock.com; p. 7 Lester Lefkowitz/Iconica/Getty Images; p. 9 (Stephen Hawking) Ian Waldie/Getty Images Entertainment/Getty Images; p. 9 (background) Universal History Archive/Universal Images Group/Getty Images; p. 11 (Gran Telescopio) https://commons.wikimedia.org/wiki/File:Grantelescopio.jpg; p. 11 (Hobby-Eberly Telescope) https://commons.wikimedia.org/wiki/File:HET_Dome.jpg; p. 11 (Keck Telescopes) https://commons.wikimedia.org/wiki/File:KeckTelescopes-hi.png; p. 11 (Large Binocular Telescope) https://commons.wikimedia.org/wiki/File:Large_Binocular_Telescope_2.jpg; p. 11 (Subaru) https://commons.wikimedia.org/wiki/File:MaunaKea_Subaru.jpg; p. 11 (Paranal Observatory) https://commons.wikimedia.org/wiki/File:Paranal_top.jpg; p. 11 (Southern African Large Telescope) https://commons.wikimedia.org/wiki/File:Southern_African_Large_Telescope_720x576px.jpg; p. 13 (ATERUI) Makoto Shizugami/Center for Computational Astrophysics/National Astronomical Observatory of Japan; p. 13 (top) https://commons.wikimedia.org/wiki/File:European_Antennas_at_ALMA%27s_Operations_Support_Facility.jpg; p. 14 https://en.wikipedia.org/wiki/File:NASA_logo.svg; p. 15 https://commons.wikimedia.org/wiki/File:International_Space_Station_after_undocking_of_STS-132.jpg; p. 17 (top) Amp/Shutterstock.com; p. 17 (bottom) https://en.wikipedia.org/wiki/File:PIA16239_High-Resolution_Self-Portrait_by_Curiosity_Rover_Arm_Camera.jpg; p. 19 (top) Hero Images/Getty Images; p. 19 (bottom) sdecoret/Shutterstock.com; p. 21 Pavel L Photo and Video/Shutterstock.com; p. 22 jirawatfoto/Shutterstock.com.

Library of Congress Cataloging-in-Publication Data

Lee, David, 1990- author.
A day at work with an astronomer / David Lee.
    pages cm. — (Super STEM careers)
Includes index.
ISBN 978-1-5081-4419-9 (pbk.)
ISBN 978-1-4994-1862-0 (6 pack)
ISBN 978-1-5081-4420-5 (library binding)
1. Astronomy—Vocational guidance—Juvenile literature. 2. Astronomers—Juvenile literature. I. Title.
QB51.5.L44 2016
520—dc23
                                2015032213

Manufactured in the United States of America

CPSIA Compliance Information: Batch #BW16PK: For Further Information contact Rosen Publishing, New York, New York at 1-800-237-9932

CONTENTS

WRITTEN IN THE STARS

Have you ever looked up at the night sky and wondered what was beyond Earth? Have you ever tried to pick out constellations, or patterns among the stars? Do you wonder what the universe is made of? If so, you might love a career as an astronomer.

Astronomers study things beyond our planet. They observe stars and other space bodies and track how they move and change. Some astronomers work in schools, while others work in **observatories**. However, all astronomers use STEM skills every day to do their work. That stands for "science, **technology**, **engineering**, and math."

Astronomers spend a lot of time **analyzing** information and teaching it to others. However, many astronomers spend plenty of time observing the sky.

THE SCIENCE OF SPACE

Astronomers are scientists who study space. Astronomy is the study of the stars, planets, and space. Astronomers try to find what certain space bodies are made of and how they change and affect things around them.

There are two kinds of astronomers. Observational astronomers study space directly. They're the scientists who use telescopes and other technology to see what's out there. They might chart the moon's craters or observe a nebula, which is a cloud of space dust. **Theoretical** astronomers mostly work on computers. They make models of bodies in space to see how space systems may have come to be.

SUPER STEM SMARTS

Astronomers often use physics in their work. Physics is a branch of science that studies matter and energy, and how they act together.

Theoretical astronomers use the information that observational astronomers collect to make their models and create **simulations**. That helps them guess what might happen in the future.

An astronomer may decide to focus on one kind of space body or space event. For example, cosmologists observe the whole universe from its beginning until now. Galactic astronomers study the galaxy we live in, which is called the Milky Way. A galaxy is a huge group of gas, dust, and billions of stars. There are many solar systems—or groups of planets moving around a sun—inside each galaxy.

Planetary astronomers focus on planets. They observe planets near and far in each stage of their life. They learn about how planets form, grow, and change.

SUPER STEM SMARTS
Some astronomers work in astrometry, which is the measuring of space bodies and their distances from one another.

Stephen Hawking is a physicist and cosmologist. He became famous for his **theories** on black holes and the beginning of the universe.

OUT-OF-THIS-WORLD TECHNOLOGY

In the early days of astronomy, people had only their own eyes to observe the night sky. Today, astronomers use advanced telescopes to observe what's happening outside our world.

Many of the biggest and most powerful telescopes in the world are in observatories. Observatories are places that hold huge telescopes and other scientific tools used to study space phenomena, or happenings. The largest telescope in the world, called the Giant Magellan Telescope, is being built for Las Campanas Observatory in Chile. However, it may not fully work until 2024. At that time, astronomers hope the telescope will unlock many mysteries of the universe.

The Gran Telescopio Canarias, or Grand Canary Telescope, sits on a peak on the island of La Palma, in the Canary Islands of Spain. It started observing space in 2009 and is the largest working telescope of its kind on Earth.

KECK 1 AND 2
Mauna Kea Observatories,
Hawaii, USA

SOUTHERN AFRICAN LARGE TELESCOPE
South African Astronomical
Observatory, Northern Cape, South Africa

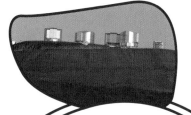

HOBBY-EBERLY TELESCOPE
McDonald Observatory,
Texas, USA

VERY LARGE TELESCOPE
(multiple)
Paranal Observatory,
Antofagasta Region, Chile

WORLD'S MOST POWERFUL TELESCOPES

SUBARU
Mauna Kea Observatories,
Hawaii, USA

GRAN TELESCOPIO CANARIAS
Roque de los Muchachos Observatory,
Canary Islands, Spain

LARGE BINOCULAR TELESCOPE
Mount Graham International
Observatory, Arizona, USA

Aside from telescopes, computers are some of the best tools astronomers have. Images from telescopes are sent straight to computers. In fact, you can see images taken by the Hubble Space Telescope online! Astronomers study these images to try to understand what's happening in space.

Computers can also simulate what happens or may happen in space. Imagine an astronomer sees an asteroid, or large space rock, zooming through space. They can observe the asteroid, create a model of it on the computer, and simulate its path. An astronomer could also look at a distant star and simulate how it will change over time.

SUPER STEM SMARTS

Supercomputers take information, or data, from telescopes and use it to do experiments to test theories on how and why something happened in space.

The National Astronomical Observatory of Japan has a supercomputer named ATERUI. Astronomers hope this computer will help expand their knowledge of space phenomena.

AEROSPACE ENGINEERING

Are you interested in both astronomy and engineering? A career as an **aerospace** engineer might be the right fit for you. Aerospace engineers **design**, build, and test things that fly. Some work on aircraft, such as airplanes and helicopters.

Astronautical engineers make things that fly through space, such as space stations and space shuttles. They need to have a strong understanding of space to choose the right **materials** to work with. They discover new ways to power the spacecraft and help it **communicate** with astronomers on Earth.

SUPER STEM SMARTS

Some aerospace engineers work for NASA, which stands for National Aeronautics and Space Administration. It's the government agency that takes care of the space program and aerospace research.

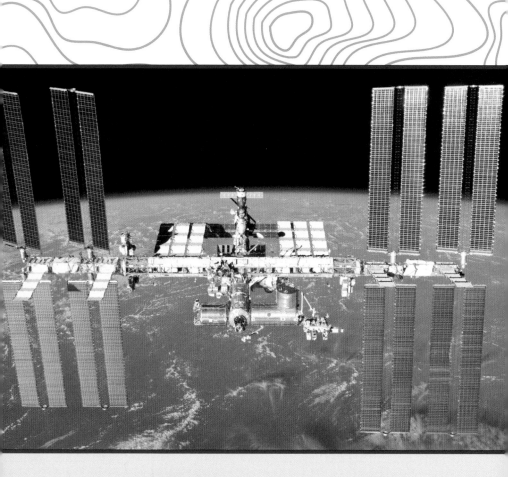

Many astronomical discoveries come from
the International Space Station (ISS).
It houses scientists and engineers who
make amazing discoveries from a research
laboratory in space.

AEROSPACE ADVANCES

Astronomers can help engineers create the best spacecraft and other technology. They can educate engineers about the materials and forces that exist in space. For example, an aerospace engineer who wants to build a new Mars rover, or unmanned **vehicle**, needs to know about Mars. An astronomer can collect and analyze data about Mars for the engineer.

Unmanned vehicles are one of the best ways we can learn about space. In 2011, the Mars rover *Curiosity* was sent to the red planet. It wanders around the planet taking pictures, which teach us about the landscape and conditions on Mars. It collects rock and soil samples, too.

SUPER STEM SMARTS

Even if astronomers don't design and build spacecraft and telescopes on their own, they're important in the creation process. They may create simulations of the space objects and phenomena that a spacecraft may encounter.

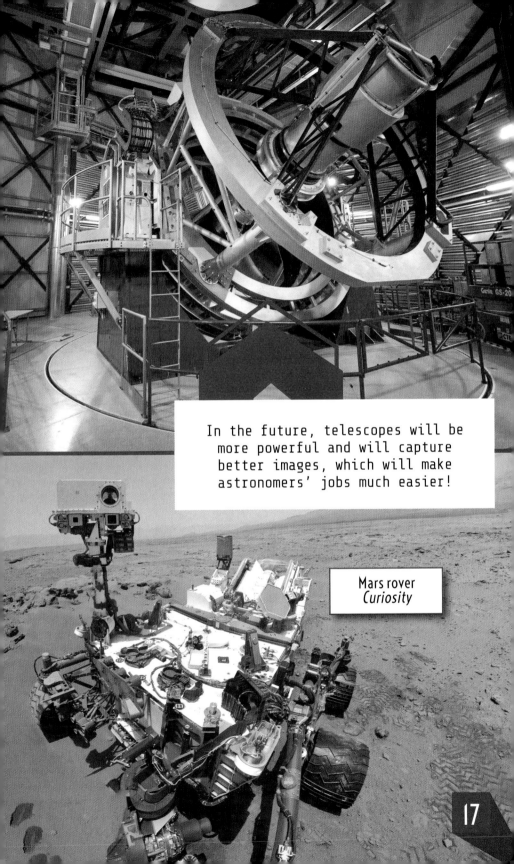

In the future, telescopes will be more powerful and will capture better images, which will make astronomers' jobs much easier!

Mars rover
Curiosity

USING MATH

Astronomers use math skills every day. That's because they discover a large amount of data in their observations. They might use measurements to find the distance between two space bodies or how large a space body is.

When an astronomer looks into a telescope, the telescope often gives them a bunch of numbers. These numbers measure how much light and what kind of light is given off by the space body they're observing.

Like many other scientists and mathematicians, astronomers use **formulas**. Formulas help show the relationship between two amounts of something.

SUPER STEM SMARTS

Statistics is a kind of math that focuses on collecting and analyzing many numbers. Statistics can help astronomers make predictions, or guesses about future events, based on what's already happened.

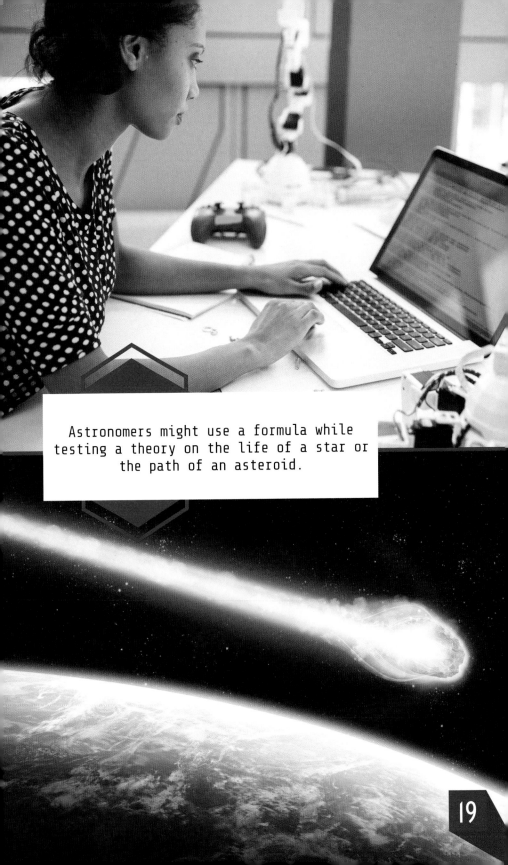

Astronomers might use a formula while testing a theory on the life of a star or the path of an asteroid.

A DAY IN THE LIFE

What do astronomers do every day? That depends on where the astronomer works. Many astronomers teach in schools and universities, or colleges. They study astronomy and teach the subject to students. If the university has an observatory, the astronomer will probably do research there or help run it.

Some astronomers work in observatories with huge telescopes. These observational astronomers spend about 10 to 30 nights a year observing space through images and telescopes. They spend the rest of their time analyzing what they've found. They make many exciting new discoveries about space!

SUPER STEM SMARTS

Some astronomers work for businesses and private **industries**. Some are hired by aerospace engineering companies to do important research.

Some astronomers work in planetariums, which are buildings where people learn about space. There's usually a rounded ceiling where images of planets and stars are shown. You can visit a planetarium to learn more about space!

EYES TO THE SKY

Astronomers spend each day learning something new. There are many mysteries about space that we'll never know the answers to. However, astronomers work tirelessly to unlock the answers to space phenomena.

How can you become an astronomer? You need at least a four-year degree in physics or astronomy to work in the field. However, most astronomers have advanced degrees in astronomy or a related field.

If you're interested in astronomy, work hard in your math and science classes, and take as many as possible. Perhaps the best thing you can do is go outside on a clear night and study the sky.

GLOSSARY

aerospace: Having to do with Earth's atmosphere and the space beyond it.

analyze: To study something deeply.

communicate: To give facts and knowledge about something to someone else.

design: To create the plan for something.

engineering: The use of science and math to build better objects.

formula: A general fact or rule expressed in letters and symbols.

industry: A group of businesses that provide a certain product or service.

material: Something used to make something else.

observatory: A special building for studying space.

simulation: A representation of a process by means of another system.

technology: The way people do something using tools and the tools that they use.

theoretical: Relating to what is possible or imagined rather than to what is known to be true or real.

theory: An idea that tries to explain something.

vehicle: An object used for carrying people or goods.

INDEX

WEBSITES

Due to the changing nature of Internet links, PowerKids Press has developed an online list of websites related to the subject of this book. This site is updated regularly. Please use this link to access the list: www.powerkidslinks.com/ssc/astro